C407800660

EARTHQUAKE
THE WORLD REACTS

Paul Bennett

Chrysalis Children's Books

27.2.04

FOREWORD

C407800660

Disasters affect everyone. At some point in your life, you have a good chance of being caught in one or of knowing somebody who is caught in one.

For most of us, the disaster may be a car crash or a house fire, and the police, fire or ambulance service will be on hand to help. But for millions of people around the world, disasters happen far more often and are more catastrophic.

Some countries suffer frequent natural disasters, such as floods, earthquakes and droughts. They do not always have the resources to deal with the crisis and it is usually the poorest people who are the most affected and least able to recover.

War is a humanmade disaster that ruins people's lives. The effects of droughts and floods are made worse when there is war.

When people find they are unable to cope with a disaster, they need the help of aid agencies, such as the Red Cross.

Aid agencies react quickly to emergencies, bringing help to those in need. Usually it is when this international aid begins to flow that you hear about a disaster in the news.

The World Reacts series ties in closely with the work of the International Federation of Red Cross and Red Crescent Societies. The Federation coordinates international disaster relief and promotes development around the world, to prevent and alleviate human suffering. There is a Red Cross or Red Crescent society in almost every country of the world. Last year we helped 22 million people caught up in disaster.

This series will help you to understand the problems faced by people threatened by disaster and to see how you can help. We hope that you enjoy these books.

George Weber
Secretary General, International Federation of Red Cross and Red Crescent Societies

SOUTH LANARKSHIRE LIBRARIES

◄ *The Red Cross symbol (left) was first created to protect the wounded in war and those who cared for them. The Red Crescent symbol (right) is used by Muslim countries around the world. Both symbols have equal status.*

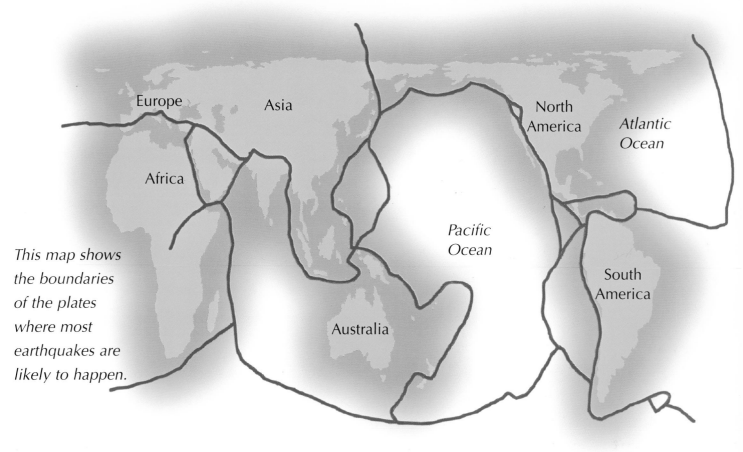

This map shows the boundaries of the plates where most earthquakes are likely to happen.

Powerful earthquakes

Earthquakes happen all the time. Every year, there are over 500 000 earthquakes around the world. But most of them are so small that no one even notices them. Large earthquakes can cause terrible damage, especially in cities and towns. Buildings and bridges collapse, roads break up and people may be killed or injured.

Scientists record earthquakes with a machine called a **seismograph**. From these readings, they use the **Richter scale** to tell the strength of an earthquake. A reading of less than two on the scale means a weak earthquake which cannot be felt. An earthquake that measures more than four can be strongly felt and those over six or seven make buildings and bridges collapse.

The world maps used in this book are Peters' projection maps. Peters' projection – named after Arno Peters who made the map – is an accurate way of seeing the world, because it shows the actual size of countries.

Aid in action

Earthquake: The World Reacts looks at what happens when an earthquake strikes. It takes examples of earthquakes from around the world and describes the help given by governments and **aid agencies.**

This book will help you understand the problems people face in the days, weeks and months after an earthquake. It will show you how the world helps earthquake victims and suggest how you too can help.

DISASTER STRIKES

During an earthquake, buildings turn to rubble and roads and bridges are destroyed.

A destructive force

The power of an earthquake is almost impossible to imagine. Millions of tonnes of rock are moved in a few seconds, and thousands of square kilometres of land may be affected by the shaking.

Earthquake damage is greatest in cities. Buildings heave up and down and their walls give way. People are crushed or trapped inside buildings as they collapse. Bricks and glass rain down on pavements and cars are bounced up and down on the road. Water and gas pipes break, and power lines fall to the ground.

People are unable to move until the shaking has stopped. Survivors who are not trapped in the rubble or badly injured start the job of searching for people buried beneath the piles of stones and bricks.

▼ *A bus balances dangerously on the edge of a collapsed bridge after an earthquake.*

Earthquake drills

People living in earthquake zones try to prepare as much as possible for disaster. For example, Japanese children carry out drills which could save their lives. To prepare for an earthquake, they are taught: to crouch under tables (above) or to seek shelter under archways or doorways; to keep away from buildings, high walls, windows and chimneys; not to re-enter damaged buildings; and to stay in a car or bus if they are travelling. They are also given disaster kits which include a bottle of water, food, a whistle, a first-aid kit, a torch and a radio.

Japan 1995
Raging fires

On 16 January 1995, the Japanese city of Kobe awoke to an earthquake. First there was a violent sideways shaking that made the ground quiver for a few seconds. Then came a **shock wave** that lasted for 20 seconds.

▲ *Fires raged in Kobe for several days until there was nothing left to burn.*

The city's houses were built in traditional Japanese style, with wooden walls and heavy, tiled roofs. When the ground shook, the roofs collapsed on the people inside, crushing many of them to death.

Leaking gas from broken pipes caught fire and set light to the wrecked wooden houses, killing many survivors. Water pipes were broken, so the emergency services couldn't put out the fires.

About 5500 people died in the earthquake and 37 000 were injured. More than 200 000 houses and buildings were damaged or destroyed.

A shopkeeper caught up in the earthquake said:

'People have lost everything and are worried about their future. They don't know how they are going to earn money or feed their families.'

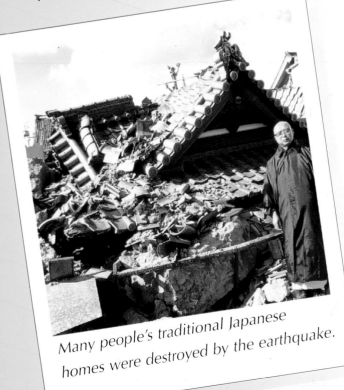

Many people's traditional Japanese homes were destroyed by the earthquake.

EMERGENCY DECLARED

After a large earthquake, the government declares an emergency and sends rescue services into the disaster area.

Chaos on the streets

Experts go to the scene of an earthquake to find out how much damage there is and to report back to the government.

Travelling to a ruined town or city may be difficult, as roads may be blocked by destroyed buildings lying across the street. Roads may have huge cracks in them, and bridges and tunnels may be destroyed.

In countries where earthquakes are common, the emergency services put a plan into action which they have practised many times. Local fire officers are joined by hundreds of firefighters from across the region. Extra doctors and nurses are brought in, and centres are set up where people can find shelter, food, water and medical help.

◀ *Firefighters at a burning building after the Los Angeles earthquake of 1994.*

Aftershocks

An earthquake is often followed by a series of aftershocks. Aftershocks are vibrations after a main earthquake, caused by the movement of rocks as they settle into their new position. Aftershocks usually become weaker and weaker, until they cannot be felt at all. They may make buildings collapse that have already been weakened by the main earthquake. This is why it is important not to enter a damaged building after an earthquake. People often prefer to camp outside until the danger from aftershocks has passed.

United States 1994

Californian quake

An earthquake measuring 6.6 on the Richter scale hit the Californian city of Los Angeles on 17 January 1994. The ground suddenly lurched upwards, causing gas mains to burst into flames, water from broken pipes to flood the streets and buildings and roads to collapse. Thousands of people were injured in the earthquake and 50 people were killed.

Within minutes, the city's mayor sent firefighters and doctors and nurses into the affected areas. A few hours later, the President, Bill Clinton, declared a **state of emergency**, and sent search-and-rescue and medical teams from all over the United States to Los Angeles.

▲ Rescue workers pull someone from the wreckage of their car after a road collapsed.

Camping out

Thousands of people camped out in parks for several nights as aftershocks continued to rock the city. The **Red Cross** set up more than 20 camps in the area, to give out bedding, free meals and water. The earthquake struck early in the morning, when most people were in bed. If it had hit a few hours later when people were driving to work, many more would have died.

◄ People camping out in a city park cook on a barbecue.

FINDING SURVIVORS

Rescue teams search under the rubble for survivors. This can be dangerous, because buildings may still collapse.

Mountains of rubble

As soon as an earthquake stops, people start looking for their families or friends trapped under piles of stones, bricks and twisted metal from fallen buildings. They use their hands to turn over the rubble in the hope of finding someone alive.

The police and army often organize the rescue effort. They are joined by ordinary people who offer to help in the search for survivors. Cranes are sometimes used in the rescue effort, mostly for lifting heavy parts of buildings, such as steel beams and slabs of concrete. Because of the danger of rubble falling on trapped people, cranes and other powerful machines are only used when there is no other way of reaching survivors.

Signs of life

People can be dug out of the rubble more quickly if rescue workers know where to dig. They use machines to detect a person's body heat and to pick up sounds from beneath the rubble. When listening devices are used, digging stops and everyone stays still and silent. Rescue teams also use trained dogs (above) in their search for survivors. Dogs have a sharp sense of smell and can work their way through the rubble, sniffing for signs of life.

◄ *A large crane is brought in to lift heavy rubble from a ruined building.*

Mexico 1985
The search for survivors

Mexico's capital, Mexico City, is built on a dried-up lake bed, made of layers of soft mud. When an earthquake hit the city in 1985, its effects were much worse because the city is built on soft ground.

The shock waves lasted for almost one minute and measured 8.1 on the Richter scale. About 10 000 people were killed and 30 000 were injured. Another 100 000 people were made homeless by the earthquake.

Rescue teams at work

The Red Cross appealed for **aid** immediately after the earthquake, and rescue teams were flown in from the United States and Europe. The teams worked day and night to find survivors. They listened in the wreckage for signs of life and used towers with powerful lights on them, so that they could carry on searching throughout the night.

▲ *Rescue workers lift an injured person from a collapsed hospital.*

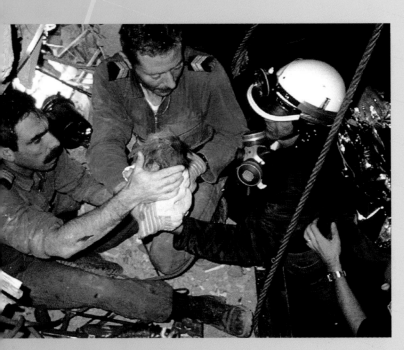

Miracle babies

Many of the city's hospitals collapsed in the earthquake, trapping patients and staff inside. Eight days after the earthquake, rescue workers found babies still alive in the ruins of the city's General Hospital.

◄ *One of the babies being rescued from the rubble of Mexico City's General Hospital.*

APPEALS FOR AID

Often poor countries do not have the resources to deal with a disaster themselves. They may appeal to foreign governments and aid agencies for help.

Coping with disaster

Wealthy countries that have frequent earthquakes, such as Japan and the United States, can afford to pay for their own rescue effort. They can supply most of the people and equipment to deal with the disaster themselves. But in poorer countries, outside help may be needed. There may be no emergency services or a shortage of doctors and nurses to treat the injured.

If the earthquake happens in the countryside or in mountainous areas, news of the disaster may take days to reach the rest of the world. Local people will have to search for survivors and treat their injured until rescue teams arrive. Roads and bridges may be poorly made or destroyed, so it may take time to transport people and supplies to the disaster area. Helicopters are often the only quick way to bring in aid.

▲ *An injured woman being treated in a makeshift hospital after an earthquake in China in 1988.*

Public response

TV cameras flash scenes of earthquake destruction around the world (left). Interviews with survivors and rescue workers help us imagine what it is like to be there. People from other countries may want to help. Aid agencies set up phone lines so that people can donate money, and collection points for people who want to donate clothes and blankets to survivors.

Armenia 1988
The world responds

Armenia is a mountainous country which was part of the former **Soviet Union.** On 7 December 1988, an earthquake measuring 6.9 on the Richter scale damaged villages, towns and cities over a huge area.

President Gorbachev, the Soviet leader at that time, promised immediate help for survivors and people trapped in the **debris**. The Soviet army used bulldozers to move rubble, and hundreds of Soviet doctors were flown in with bandages and medicines. But outside help was also needed and the Soviet government appealed to the world for aid.

The relief effort

In response, aid supplies were flown in from many different countries. These included French **sniffer dogs**, German cranes and Italian shelters for the homeless.

The winter weather did not help the rescue effort. As the temperature dropped and icy rain began to fall, fewer and fewer people were brought out alive from ruined buildings. The disaster killed 25 000 people and half a million were made homeless.

▲ *President Gorbachev, second left, speaks to a crowd of survivors in northern Armenia.*

▼ *Hundreds of Soviet soldiers were sent to Armenia to help the relief effort. Here, soldiers are unloading food supplies from the back of an army truck.*

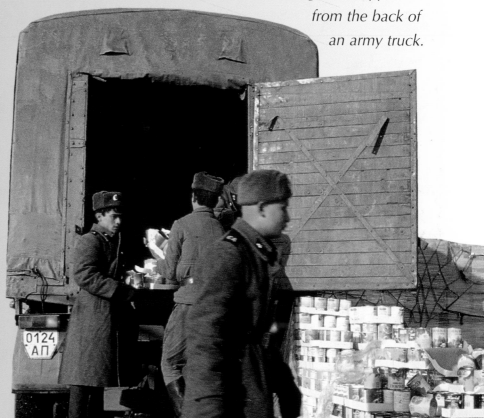

THE RELIEF EFFORT

Aid agencies react quickly to a disaster. They ship relief items to the affected area within hours of hearing about a crisis.

Help at hand

Aid agencies help people around the world caught up in disasters such as earthquakes. They are also involved in **development** work to give people long-term help.

Often aid agencies already have aid workers in a country when it is hit by an earthquake. These workers travel quickly to the area, assess the damage, then report back to their central office, giving details of the people and supplies that are needed. People may be hurt, so medicines and doctors and nurses are needed to treat their injuries. Homes may be destroyed, so tents are sent in to house the homeless, along with blankets and clothes to keep people warm.

◄ *This makeshift shelter became home to these children and their cat after the Mexico City earthquake of 1985.*

Airdropping aid

It is important to transport relief supplies quickly to the affected area. This can be difficult in mountainous regions or if weather conditions are bad.

Large planes, such as the **Hercules**, can carry between 25 and 30 tonnes of aid supplies in one airlift. If there are no good places to land, planes may fly in low and drop supplies by parachute.

Helicopters (above) and small planes can often land in remote areas that large planes find difficult to reach. But they can only carry small loads – 700 kg at the most – and have space for only six people.

Afghanistan 1998
Flying in aid

An earthquake measuring 6.1 on the Richter scale hit the northern Rustaq area of Afghanistan on 4 February 1998. It was followed by several aftershocks which caused more damage. Aid agencies estimate that as many as 4500 people died.

An international appeal was made as soon as news of the earthquake reached the rest of the world. Aid agencies, including the **United Nations (UN)**, the Red Cross and **Médecins Sans Frontières**, helped in the relief effort. But their work was made difficult by heavy snowfall in this mountainous region.

▲ *Villagers lead their donkeys through a snow storm to deliver sacks of wheat to earthquake survivors.*

▼ *A UN plane delivers clothes and blankets for the homeless.*

Moving supplies

The main problem was moving aid supplies. Many of the roads were bad, so aid agencies used over 200 donkeys to carry supplies to more remote villages.

The United Nations and the Red Cross also used planes to drop supplies of tents, plastic sheeting, medicine and clothes to the homeless who were left outside in the bitter cold. But many of the airlifts were slowed down by bad weather, and people had to wait for supplies to arrive.

THE RISK OF DISEASE

After an earthquake, water supplies become dirty and rubbish piles up in the streets. Disease can spread quickly in these unclean conditions.

Providing clean water

During an earthquake, water pipes are often broken. Water supplies may be contaminated by **sewage**, making water undrinkable. Survivors need clean drinking water to prevent the spread of diseases that are sometimes carried in dirty water.

In areas at risk from earthquakes, people often store clean water in plastic containers in case supplies are cut off. That way they have their own drinking water.

Aid agencies send in engineers to set up emergency water supplies. If necessary, they dig new wells and supply water pumps, pipes and tanks for holding the water. If this is not possible, then water has to be shipped in from another part

▲ *Water gushes down the streets as pipes burst after the Los Angeles earthquake in 1994.*

of the country. If public toilets are broken and sewage cannot be flushed away, engineers build new ones.

Health matters

Hospitals may be damaged or destroyed during an earthquake. Aid agencies, such as the Red Cross and Médecins Sans Frontières, set up centres where survivors can get medical help. People are given injections to prevent them catching diseases. Health experts advise on burying people killed in the disaster. They also make sure that rubbish is cleared away or burned.

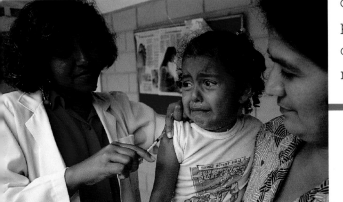

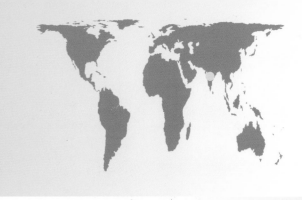

India 1993
Dirty waters

On 30 September 1993, the Latur region of central India was rocked by an earthquake that measured 6.4 on the Richter scale. It destroyed more than 100 villages, killed 8000 people and left 150 000 people homeless. The earthquake happened during the night, and many sleeping villagers were buried alive when their homes collapsed on top of them.

The Indian army led the rescue effort. Medical teams and ambulances were sent to the region and thousands of tents were put up to house survivors. Heavy rain made it difficult to rescue people trapped in the rubble. The rain also dirtied water supplies, bringing the risk of killer diseases, such as **cholera** and **typhoid**.

▲ *Homeless villagers put up shelters to house their families.*

Preventing disease

The army brought in tankers of fresh drinking water and doctors and nurses gave vaccinations to protect people from diseases.

Dr Lohinya from Manavlok, an Indian aid agency, described the earthquake:

'Killari village was at the centre of the earthquake. The devastation was beyond belief. The whole village was destroyed and there were bodies everywhere. We tried to move them and to help people trapped in the debris.'

A Killari man sits in front of the ruin that was once his home.

TSUNAMI DISASTER

An underwater earthquake can create gigantic waves which cross the oceans at incredible speed and pound the shores of countries thousands of kilometres away.

Walls of water

Tsunamis are long, high sea waves caused by underwater earthquakes. An earthquake on the sea bed sets off a series of waves that spread out in all directions. Where the water is deep, these waves are only a metre or so high. But as they reach shallow water near the coast, they become huge walls of water up to 60 metres high.

Tsunamis travel at high speeds of up to 700 kilometres per hour. A tsunami can be made up of a series of waves 160 kilometres across and may come ashore over an hour after an earthquake.

As a tsunami crashes on the shore, it carries boats inland and washes away anything in its path. It causes more damage as it washes debris back out to sea.

Tsunami warnings

The Pacific Tsunami Warning Centre in Hawaii monitors earthquakes in the Pacific Ocean. Its scientists use computers to find out how big a tsunami is likely to be and how quickly it will reach the shore. They use tsunami buoys (above) to monitor wave movements. Warnings are given to countries around the Pacific which are likely to be affected, so that people in coastal areas can move inland.

◀ *A tsunami in Alaska in 1964 crushed homes over a wide area.*

18

Okushiri Island 1993

Taken by surprise

There are more earthquakes around the rim of the Pacific Ocean than anywhere else on Earth. Scientists monitor these earthquakes and can give warnings of tsunamis as they move across the Pacific.

But if an earthquake happens close to the shore, people living on the coast have little time to escape from a tsunami – as the people of Okushiri Island in the Sea of Japan found out late one night in July 1993.

Running for cover

An underwater earthquake measuring 7.8 on the Richter scale struck just 55 kilometres off the coast of the island. The island's people – aware of the danger of tsunamis in the region – ran out of their homes to warn their neighbours to move inland. But just four minutes later, there was a roaring sound and a wall of water thundered ashore.

▲ *Even the island's lighthouse was damaged by the tsunami as it came ashore.*

It was pitch dark and hundreds of people were caught by the wave. Eight minutes later, a second wave struck, causing more damage. Then the sea – now full of wrecked fishing boats and debris from houses – became calm again.

A sea wall has been built to protect the island from high sea waves, but the people of Okushiri Island know that the best way to escape a tsunami is to run inland.

◄ *Fishing boats destroyed by the tsunami.*

SLIDING LAND

Earthquakes can move huge amounts of earth, sending rocks crashing down mountain slopes at amazing speeds.

Rivers of soil

A violent earthquake shakes soil and rock loose on hill and mountain sides. The soil then begins to flow down the slope. This is called a landslide.

As the landslide moves downhill, it gathers speed and weight. It picks up stones, tree trunks and rubble from destroyed buildings along the way. These rivers of soil and debris are very powerful. They cause lots of damage and can kill thousands of people.

Large landslides can swallow up whole towns and villages, burying people beneath the mud. When this happens, emergency rescue teams are sent into the area to try to dig people out alive.

Roads and railway lines cut into hill sides may be covered with soil and rock, making it difficult to reach survivors. Bulldozers are often used to clear roads so that rescue workers can get through.

Preventing damage

Areas at risk from landslides can be identified to help prevent damage. In these high-risk areas, it may be possible to predict the path a landslide will take and so take steps to avoid disaster.

Once the likely path is known, channels can be built to direct the flow away from a town or village. Strong barriers can also be built across a hillside to stop a landslide before it starts. Underground drainage systems drain away excess water that sometimes causes landslides on unstable slopes.

But all these measures cost money – money that poorer countries cannot always afford.

◄ *A landslide of mud, sand and uprooted trees swept through this village, causing much damage.*

Peru 1970
A buried town

Yungay was a small town at the foot of Peru's highest mountain, Huascarán. The mountain is 6768 metres high and is part of the Andes range, which runs along the west coast of South America.

In May 1970, an earthquake off the coast of Peru triggered an **avalanche** from the top of Huascarán. Snow and rock plunged down the mountain at more than 300 kilometres per hour. Melting ice mixed with soil to form a fast-flowing river of mud.

▲ Yungay covered in mud. In the distance is Huascarán, where the landslide began.

▲ The cemetery where Yungay's only survivors were found.

Buried alive!

The mudflow took just six minutes to reach Yungay in the valley below. Nearly 18 000 people were buried alive, as the giant river of mud and debris swallowed up the town.

When rescue teams arrived at the scene, they realized there was nothing they could do. There was no point in trying to dig people out of the mud, because no one could have survived the disaster.

But there were some survivors. Two hundred people had run to the cemetery, the town's highest point, and were saved.

THE HUMAN COST

After an earthquake, people suffer from shock. They find it very hard to believe what has happened.

Picking up the pieces

It may take years for people to rebuild their lives and return to normal after an earthquake. Their homes are destroyed and many may have lost family and friends. The homeless need somewhere to live before they can start picking up the pieces of their lives.

Gas mains, water pipes, electricity cables and phone lines have to be repaired, as well as roads, railways and bridges. Schools, offices and factories that are still standing are closed until they are judged safe to enter.

Many survivors find it difficult to return to a normal life after an earthquake, especially if their family or friends died in the disaster. Aid agencies send specially-trained people called counsellors to help survivors cope with feelings of shock and **grief**.

Manmade earthquakes?

Humans can cause small earthquakes when they build dams. This is because the weight of the water in a dam makes rocks shift in a movement similar to an earthquake. The Hoover Dam in the USA (above), the Koyna Dam in India and the Kariba Dam in Africa have all caused earth tremors. Most of the shocks have been very weak, but some of them have measured as much as five on the Richter scale.

◀ *This man lost his home after an earthquake in Iran in 1990.*

Italy 1997
Damage to art treasures

In September 1997, a series of earthquakes hit several small towns in central Italy. The tremors were not very violent, but they damaged buildings and caused six deaths. One of the towns affected was Assisi, the birthplace of St Francis, a Christian who founded a religious order almost 800 years ago.

The Catholic Church in Assisi, called the Basilica of Assisi, was one of the buildings damaged in the earthquake. The Basilica had many paintings on its walls by Giotto, a famous fourteenth-century artist. The paintings, or frescoes, were either cracked or totally destroyed. Art experts all over the world were shocked, because the frescoes were priceless.

◀ *Many of the Basilica of Assisi's valuable frescoes were destroyed when the earthquake struck.*

While the frescoes were being examined, part of the Basilica's roof caved in, killing four people. A newspaper photographer who was inside the Basilica at the time said:

'Suddenly there was a violent shock. All I could see when I recovered was a thick cloud of dust inside the church. When it cleared, I saw the bodies of the people who had been killed.'

A photographer captured the Basilica's roof caving in on film.

23

COUNTING THE COST

It is expensive to rebuild a city after an earthquake. Rich countries can afford these costs, but poor countries may not have the money to fund rebuilding.

Finding the money

The cost of rebuilding after the Kobe earthquake in 1995 was about £31 billion. Repair costs after the Los Angeles earthquake in 1994 came to £6 billion.

These are huge amounts of money for any country to find. But for a poor country, the cost of rebuilding a city can plunge it into deeper poverty. The government may have to borrow money from foreign banks. But this money has to be paid back within a certain period of time and with an extra amount, called interest, paid on top.

Aid agencies help with local rebuilding projects by supplying the materials that local people need. Engineers and **architects** give advice on making damaged buildings safe again and on building homes that will stand up to future earthquakes.

◀ An architect advises on the rebuilding of houses after the Mexican earthquake in 1985.

Earthquake-proof buildings

Buildings can be specially designed to withstand the swaying of an earthquake. This is important for reducing damage in cities, such as Tokyo and San Francisco, which are particularly at risk from earthquakes. All buildings should be built on solid rock or with firm foundations. Light roofs cause less damage when they fall than heavy, tiled roofs. Many modern skyscrapers are built with lightweight materials supported by a strong steel frame which bends in an earthquake but will not collapse.

Ecuador 1987

Rebuilding lives

On a cold night in March 1987, a violent earthquake shook the South American country of Ecuador. Fifteen thousand homes were destroyed and many hundreds of people were killed or injured.

Ecuador found itself in a deep crisis. It is a poor country and needed outside help to cope with the disaster. With the help of the United Nations (UN), local people in the highland and rainforest areas of Ecuador began rebuilding their lives.

The UN worked closely with local people to build new homes that would stand up better to the violent shaking of an earthquake.

▲ *A woman stands in front of the ruins of her home after the earthquake in Ecuador.*

▼ *The earthquake destroyed this bridge and ripped through a nearby oil pipeline.*

Safer homes

Most of the houses in the area had been built without any beams at the base of the roof. This meant that during the earthquake, the weight of the roofs had pushed the walls outwards, making the houses fall apart. All new houses were built using local **eucalyptus trees** as pillars to support the roofs. These pillars were both strong and flexible, making houses safer.

This rebuilding project meant that any future earthquakes would cause less damage to people's homes.

PREVENTING DISASTER

Countries can prepare for earthquakes by making emergency plans. These plans guide the rescue services and identify the areas most at risk.

Emergency plans

Earthquakes cannot be prevented and it is difficult to predict them. But the numbers of people killed and injured can be reduced if everyone is prepared.

People in earthquake zones make emergency action plans to prepare for disaster. These plans include how the fire, police and ambulance services will react, how the rescue operation will be carried out, and the role the army will play.

Some cities have automatic systems to cut off gas and electricity if an earthquake strikes. This helps to reduce the risk of fire. Water for fighting fires is stored in underground tanks in case water pipes are broken.

▲ *An emergency earthquake exercie in the city of Caracas in Venezuela, South America.*

Decade for Disaster Reduction

At the United Nations, the countries of the world are working together to reduce the damage and destruction caused by natural disasters, such as earthquakes. They have declared the 1990s the International Decade for Natural Disaster Reduction. The United Nations works closely with governments, aid agencies, universities and schools to make sure that people know what to do if their area is hit by a natural disaster.

New Guinea 1998

Plans to save lives

The islands of the South Pacific are often threatened by natural disasters, such as earthquakes and volcanic eruptions. This is because many of them are on the edges of the Earth's plates and are part of **volcanic island** chains. The islands of New Guinea in the South West Pacific have suffered many earthquakes and volcanic eruptions. In 1996, for example, an earthquake measuring 7.2 on the Richter scale caused much destruction and triggered a huge tsunami. Eighty-four people were killed on New Guinea and the surrounding islands.

▲ *A man and his son bury a member of their family killed by the tsunami.*

▼ *This boat was swept ashore by the large waves that were triggered by the earthquake.*

Preparing for disaster

To cope with these and other natural disasters, the New Guinea government has worked with the United Nations and other Pacific countries on emergency plans to prepare for disaster.

Many of the plans are organized by local people. People know what to do if disaster strikes and regularly practise emergency drills which could save their lives.

PREDICTING QUAKES

Millions of pounds are spent every year on earthquake research. But scientists still do not know where earthquakes will hit or how to control them.

Changes in the ground

Japan and the United States are world leaders in developing new technology to predict earthquakes. Scientists use satellites, lasers and machines called strain meters to detect rock movements. Survey satellites in space have sensitive instruments that can measure large rock movements. Smaller movements are measured by strain meters which are positioned in the ground across fault lines. But scientists are still far from being able to predict earthquakes and give earthquake warnings.

People in Japan and California live in fear of 'the big one' striking their homes – a massive earthquake that would kill hundreds of thousands of people. Scientists say that such an earthquake is overdue and that it is only a matter of time before it comes.

Animal antics

An ancient way of predicting earthquakes is to observe changes in animal behaviour. If animals appear nervous, this is a sign that an earthquake is coming.

The ancient Chinese used a device which held tiny balls over the open mouths of statues of frogs (above). Even the slightest tremor would make the balls drop. Anyone who found a ball in a frog's mouth would know that an earthquake was coming.

◄ Laser beams measure tiny rock movements along California's San Andreas Fault.

China 1998
Out in the cold

On 10 January 1998, an earthquake struck Hebei, a region in northern China, killing 50 people and injuring more than 10 000. The earthquake measured 6.2 on the Richter scale and destroyed more than 100 000 homes across the province.

The Chinese army rescued people trapped under the rubble and medical teams were sent in from all over the country. The government appealed for help to cope with the disaster, and aid agencies, such as the Red Cross and OXFAM, sent tents, blankets, food and warm clothes to the people of Hebei.

The relief effort was made difficult by the freezing weather. The temperature dropped to -25°C during the day and there were fresh falls of snow.

▲ *Chinese soldiers erect a tent to be used as a shelter for earthquake survivors.*

Eight people lived in this temporary tent after the Hebei earthquake in 1998.

Many people made homeless by the earthquake had to huddle around fires in the open air until buildings had been examined and judged safe to enter.

A peasant woman, Zhang Yu-e, described the difficult conditions:

'It was too cold to work outside and we could not rebuild our house immediately. We had to stay inside the temporary tent.'

HOW YOU CAN HELP

Earthquakes can strike at any time. They hit countries both rich and poor, large and small.

● Look closely at the map on page 5 which shows the boundaries of the Earth's plates. Using an atlas, note down the countries in the world that are most at risk from earthquakes.

● Collect newspaper cuttings about earthquakes. How strong were the earthquakes and how much damage did they cause? Did aid agencies send relief supplies to the country?

● Imagine that earthquakes are common where you live. Work with your friends to prepare for disaster. Write out a plan of action to help injured people and to provide survivors with food, shelter and water.

● Have a look at the 'Earthquake drills' fact box on page 6. Make a poster to warn people what they should do if an earthquake strikes.

● Choose an aid agency you would like to raise money for. Organize a fundraising activity, such as a sponsored run or swim. Design your own sponsorship form and give information about how the money will be spent and who it will help.

Finding out more

Write to aid agencies or visit their web sites to find out about their work and how you can help.

British Red Cross
9 Grosvenor Crescent
London SW1X 7EJ
Telephone: 0171 235 5454
http://www.redcross.org.uk

OXFAM
274 Banbury Road
Oxford OX2 7DZ
Telephone: 01865 313600
http://www.oxfam.org.uk

Save the Children Fund (SCF)
17 Grove Lane
London SE5 8RD
Telephone: 0171 703 5400
http://www.oneworld.org/scf/

ACTIONAID
Hamlyn House
Macdonald Road
Archway
London N19 5PG
Telephone: 0171 281 4101
http://www.oneworld.org/actionaid

Médecins Sans Frontières (MSF)
124–132 Clerkenwell Road
London EC1R 5DL
Telephone: 0171 713 5600
http://www.msf.org

The Office for the Coordination of Humanitarian Affairs (helps victims of man-made and natural disasters)
United Nations
New York NY10017
USA
http://www.un.org

The International Federation of Red Cross and Red Crescent Societies
17 chemin des Crêts
Petit-Saconnex
PO Box 372
CH-1211
Geneva 19
Switzerland
Telephone: 00 41 22 730 4222
http://www.ifrc.org

GLOSSARY

aid Resources given by one country, or organization, to another country. Aid is given to help people in an emergency and to improve their lives in the longer term.

aid agency An organization that helps people when there is a disaster and runs long-term projects to help people in poorer countries.

architect Someone who designs buildings and supervises their construction.

avalanche A huge mass of snow, ice and soil that falls down a mountain side at high speed, causing much damage.

cholera A very infectious disease usually caused by drinking dirty water. Cholera can end in death.

debris The remains of a destroyed building. Another word for rubble.

development The use of resources in a country to increase the standard of living of its people.

eucalyptus tree Trees that produce a gum, called kino. Also called gum trees. The wood from eucalyptus trees is used for building homes in some parts of the world.

fault A crack or fracture in the Earth's crust. The rocks on one or both sides of a fault may slip up or down. Most faults are inactive, but some move quite regularly, causing earthquakes.

grief Deep sorrow, especially when someone dies.

Hercules A type of large plane designed for transporting heavy loads.

Médecins Sans Frontières (MSF) An aid agency which offers medical help in a crisis. The name is French for 'doctors without borders'.

plates The sections of the Earth's crust. Fault lines are found at the edges of the plates. Most earthquakes happen where the plates meet.

Red Cross An international aid agency which was set up in 1863. Its symbol is a red cross.

Richter scale A scale for measuring the size of an earthquake by the amount of energy released. The scale goes from 0 to over 8. This scale was invented by the American scientist, Charles M. Richter.

San Andreas Fault A huge crack in the Earth's crust that runs along the west coast of the USA. It is nearly 965 kilometres long. Many earthquakes happen here.

seismograph An instrument used for recording earth movements. The pattern of these movements can be used to tell the strength and duration of an earthquake.

sewage Waste material and liquid from houses and factories that is carried away by drains or sewers. Sewage can cause serious illnesses if it gets into water supplies.

shock wave Violent vibrations from an earthquake that cause lots of damage in a very short period of time.

sniffer dog A dog that is specially trained to use its keen sense of smell to find people trapped under rubble.

Soviet Union A large country in Eastern Europe and Asia, made up of many different states. The Soviet Union split apart in 1991.

state of emergency A situation where a government declares that urgent measures must be taken to provide aid for disaster victims.

typhoid A disease caused by drinking dirty water or eating contaminated food. Typhoid can be treated.

United Nations (UN) An organization of countries around the world which encourages world peace and offers help to people in a crisis.

volcanic island An island that has been formed by the eruption of an underwater volcano. The lava that comes out of the volcano slowly builds up a mountain under the sea, which grows each time the volcano erupts, until it appears above sea level as an island.

INDEX

First published in Great Britain in 1999 by

Chrysalis Children's Books
An imprint of Chrysalis Books Group plc
The Chrysalis Building, Bramley Road,
London W10 6SP

Copyright in this format © Chrysalis Books Group plc 1999
Text copyright © Paul Bennet 1999

Paperback edition published in 2003

Series editor Julie Hill
Series designer Simeen Karim
Consultants Dr Peter Walker and Elizabeth Bassant
Picture researcher Diana Morris

All rights reserved. No part of this book may be reproduced or utilised in any form or by any means, electronic or mechanical, including photocopying, recording or by any information storage and retrieval system, without permission in writing from the publisher, except by a reviewer who may quote brief passages in a review.

ISBN 1 85561 810 9 (hb)
ISBN 1 84138 950 1 (pb)

British Library Cataloguing in Publication Data for this book is available from the British Library.

Printed in Hong Kong

Photographic credits

Andes Press Agency/Caretas: 21b. N. Blickov/Camera Press: front cover. British Red Cross: 3, 11t, 14b & 24 L. de Toledo. Camera Press: 6t. Jungkwam Chi/Camera Press: 5t. Jerome Delay/AP photo: 14t, 15t, 15b. Marc Deville/Gamma/Frank Spooner: 17b. Dinodia/Camera Press: 17t. Gaillarde/Gamma/Frank Spooner: 10b. Garnikian/Sipa/Rex Features: 13b. P. J. Griffiths/Magnum: 5b. Benoit Gysembergh/Camera Press: 10t. Haley/Sipa/Rex Features: 11b. David Hoffmann/Still Pictures: 20b. Hokkaido/Gamma/Frank Spooner: 19t, 19b. Michael Holford: 28t. Jeremy Horner/Panos: 16b. ICRC: 2. IFRC: 1 Damien Personnaz. ITAR/Camera Press: 13t. W. Janoud/Powerstock/Zefa: 21t. Paul Kennedy/Gamma-Liaison/Frank Spooner: 12b. T. Litsios/Gamma-Liaison/Frank Spooner: 8b. S. McCutcheon/ FLPA: 18b. Mingasson/Gamma-Liaison/Frank Spooner: 8t. NOAA/AP photo: 18t. Oxfam Hong Kong: 29b. D. Parker/SPL: 28b. Edward Parker/Still Pictures: 25t, 25b. G. Peress/Magnum: 26, 30. Eslami Rad/Gamma/Frank Spooner: 22b. Rex Features: 6b, 22t, 23b. Patrick Robert/Sygma: back cover, 4. Andrea Ruggeri/Massimo Sestini/Rex Features: 23t. Sipa/Rex Features: 7. UNHCR: 20t. Jeff Werner/Incredible Features/Rex Features: 16t. Xinhua/AP photo: 29t. Zhu Yuhu/Camera Press: 12t. Muchtar Zakaria/AP photo: 27t, 27b.

With thanks to the following for help with case study material: ACTIONAID p17; OXFAM Hong Kong p29; United Nations p25.